DATE DUE

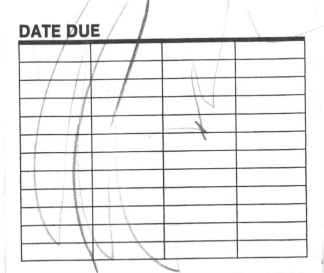

FRANKLIN
PIERCE

PRESIDENTIAL ✦ LEADERS

FRANKLIN PIERCE

CAROLINE EVENSEN LAZO

TWENTY-FIRST CENTURY BOOKS/MINNEAPOLIS

In memory of Ena Adamson Pierce

Acknowledgments:
Special thanks to Rita M. Breton and Polly B. Johnson at the Pierce Brigade and the Hillsboro
Historical Society, Hillsboro, New Hampshire, for their cooperation and assistance with this project

Many thanks to Mary Winget for her careful editing and helpful advice

Twenty-First Century Books
A division of Lerner Publishing Group
241 First Avenue North
Minneapolis, MN 55401 U.S.A.

Website address: www.lernerbooks.com

Library of Congress Cataloging-in-Publication Data

Lazo, Caroline Evensen.
    Franklin Pierce / by Caroline Evensen Lazo.
        p.   cm. — (Presidential leaders)
    Includes bibliographical references and index.
    ISBN-13: 978-0-8225-1492-3 (lib. bdg. : alk. paper)
    ISBN-10: 0-8225-1492-3 (lib. bdg. : alk. paper)
    1. Pierce, Franklin, 1804–1869— Juvenile literature. 2. Presidents—United States—
Biography—Juvenile literature. I. Title. II. Series.
    E432.L39 2007
    973.6'6092—dc22   2006005066

Manufactured in the United States of America
1 2 3 4 5 6 – JR – 12 11 10 09 08 07

CONTENTS

———— ✧ ————

Franklin Pierce in 1852

INTRODUCTION

*I have been borne to a position so suitable for
others rather than desirable for myself.*
—Franklin Pierce, from his 1853 inaugural address

No one was more surprised to become the Democratic Party's nominee for president of the United States than Franklin Pierce. He didn't campaign for the nomination. And he had no desire to become president. In fact, at the time of the party's convention in 1852, he had already resigned from the U.S. Senate and given up his busy life in Washington, D.C. He wanted to focus on his family and to practice law in the New Hampshire countryside.

Pierce liked being a country lawyer. As a loyal Democrat, he also enjoyed helping New Hampshire candidates win elections. Such activities helped him cope with the personal tragedies that haunted his life. His firstborn son, Franklin Jr., died in infancy. A few years later, his second son, Franklin Robert, died of typhus. Pierce's wife Jane never fully recovered from the losses. Pierce was determined to make her life as peaceful as possible—even if it meant giving up his political career.

Pierce was only thirty-eight years old when he retired. Still, he had served as both a representative to the New Hampshire legislature and as a U.S. senator. His combination of good looks, intelligence, and charm captured the hearts of New Hampshire voters and colleagues. People continued to ask him to run again for the Senate. But Pierce, in his usual polite manner, continued to say no.

Finally, in 1852, longtime friend Edmund Burke pleaded with Pierce. Would he please allow his name to be placed in nomination for the presidency at the Democratic Party convention? Pierce said yes—but only if no other candidate could win enough votes. He was sure that such a situation would never happen. He was sure that the convention would have

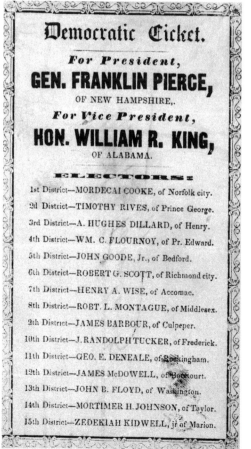

Democratic Cicket.

For President,

GEN. FRANKLIN PIERCE,

OF NEW HAMPSHIRE,.

For Vice President,

HON. WILLIAM R. KING,

OF ALABAMA.

ELECTORS:

1st District—MORDECAI COOKE, of Norfolk city.

2d District—TIMOTHY RIVES, of Prince George.

3rd District—A. HUGHES DILLARD, of Henry.

4th District—WM. C. FLOURNOY, of Pr. Edward.

5th District—JOHN GOODE, Jr., of Bedford.

6th District—ROBERT G. SCOTT, of Richmond city.

7th District—HENRY A. WISE, of Accomac.

8th District—ROBT. L. MONTAGUE, of Middlesex.

9th District—JAMES BARBOUR, of Culpeper.

10th District—J. RANDOLPH TUCKER, of Frederick.

11th District—GEO. E. DENEALE, of Rockingham.

12th District—JAMES McDOWELL, of Botetourt.

13th District—JOHN B. FLOYD, of Washington.

14th District—MORTIMER H. JOHNSON, of Taylor.

15th District—ZEDEKIAH KIDWELL, jr of Marion.

✦ ─────────

Pierce and his running mate, William R. King, were the Democratic candidates for president and vice president in 1852.

no problem selecting a nominee from the list of well-known candidates. After all, they had campaigned hard for the nomination. Jane Pierce prayed he was right.

But the convention became deadlocked. There was no clear winner. Franklin Pierce, the dark horse in the race, became the party's nominee. Though stunned by the nomination, Pierce went on to defeat General Winfield Scott in the presidential election on November 2, 1852.

Until his nomination, Pierce's name was little known outside New Hampshire. Suddenly, all Americans looked to him for leadership. And many wondered if Pierce, the peacemaker, could resolve the growing conflict between the North and the South over slavery.

Those who had known him from childhood never doubted his ability to govern the nation. But it was impossible to foresee how family problems would affect his presidency.

Franklin Pierce grew up in this large
frame house in Hillsborough, New Hampshire.

CHAPTER ONE

EARLY LESSONS

*I can express no better hope for my country
than that the kind of Providence which smiled
upon our fathers may enable their children to
preserve the blessings they have inherited.*

—Franklin Pierce, from his 1853 inaugural address

Franklin Pierce was born on November 23, 1804, in a log cabin in Hillsborough, New Hampshire. After his birth, the family moved to a large frame house in Hillsborough. The new house could accommodate the growing Pierce family. Franklin had four brothers and three sisters. While growing up there, Franklin dreamed of being a soldier—a strong, self-confident soldier like his father, General Benjamin Pierce. General Pierce had fought in the American Revolution (1775–1783). He had even won praise from General George Washington. General Pierce's children loved his stories of heroic battles for U.S. independence from Great Britain. He hoped the stories would show his children the importance of serving one's

Franklin's parents, Benjamin (left) and Anna (right) Pierce, had eight children. Franklin was the seventh child.

country—in peacetime as well as war. After serving in the American Revolution, General Pierce returned to farming. He also served as a city councilman, sheriff, and brigadier general of New Hampshire's militia (citizen army). Finally, he was selected governor of the state. His years of public service made a lasting impression on Franklin. The boy's mother, Anna Kendrick Pierce, had a profound influence on him too—but in a different way. Mrs. Pierce was easygoing, affectionate, and softhearted. She was lively and fun but also moody. According to local gossip, she "sought refuge in alcoholic stimulant." As biographer Roy Nichols noted:

> *These parents were not an ideal couple to discipline a pranky boy, for between his father's strictness and his mother's easy-going ways there was sure to be a chance for the quick-witted to escape many of the consequences of boyish disobedience.*

AT HOME WITH POLITICS

The Pierce household was a lively one, especially when all the children—Benjamin, Charles, John, Henry, Franklin, Betsey, Harriet, and Nancy—were home at the same time. Part of the large house served as a tavern. It became a popular meeting place for travelers on horseback as they made their way to Concord, New Hampshire's capital. Concord was only about six miles away. A great mix of people and wide-ranging topics of conversation filled Franklin Pierce's early life.

The main topic of conversation at the Pierces' house was politics. And no one loved to discuss politics more than General Pierce. He was a loyal member of the Democratic-Republican Party. The party believed in giving more power to individual states and less to the federal government.

The Democratic-Republican's main rival was the Federalist Party, which believed that a strong central government should offer services to those in need. Both parties claimed that their interpretations of the U.S. Constitution were correct. Like his father, Franklin followed the Democratic-Republican Party's view. He was grateful to his father for the firsthand, home-taught history lessons. But his childhood was not *all* about government issues and practices. He spent much time enjoying the outdoors with his brothers and sisters.

Franklin loved to go fishing in the small lakes near the Pierce farm. He joined his brothers in reenacting some of the Revolutionary War scenes described by their father. The boys turned the open fields into make-believe battle sites. But when Franklin was eight years old, a real war with Great Britain broke out, the War of 1812 (1812–1815). The United States declared war on Great Britain after Britain seized sailors

HISTORIC NEW HAMPSHIRE

New Hampshire, Franklin Pierce's beloved home state, was one of the original thirteen colonies. Captain Martin Pring, an Englishman, was the first explorer in the area in 1603. Samuel de Champlain, a Frenchman, followed in 1605. The region was settled by English colonists and became a royal province in 1679. New Hampshire was the first colony to declare its independence from Great Britain on January 5, 1776. New Hampshire's motto—Live Free or Die—seems appropriate.

New Hampshire became a state in 1788. It is one of the six New England states in the northeastern United States. Its many streams and lakes provided good fishing for the Abenaki Indians, the earliest people to settle there. The state's famous White Mountains contain the Northeast's highest peak, Mount Washington. It is 6,288 feet high.

New Hampshire became an important manufacturing center. The state was known for its cotton mills, paper products, and machinery. Many of its factories were located along the Merrimack and Connecticut rivers and the Atlantic Ocean.

The city of Concord, New Hampshire, in 1853,
as it appeared in the Illustrated News.

from U.S. ships and blocked U.S. shipping. During the war, General Pierce went to Concord to serve as an adviser to the governor of New Hampshire, John T. Gilman.

PREPARING FOR COLLEGE

Franklin's older brothers served in the war. Franklin wanted to join them, but he was only eight years old. Young Franklin Pierce stayed at home and finished his schooling at the local schoolhouse in Hillsborough. Then he went on to attend boarding school at Hancock Academy.

One Sunday, while in boarding school in Hancock, twelve-year-old Franklin became homesick. He decided to sneak out and go home—running as fast as he could. When he got there, the family was in church. When they later discovered Franklin at home, they didn't seem surprised. Franklin expected punishment and was amazed to receive none. General Pierce even invited Franklin for a ride in the family's carriage. The boy was delighted. But about halfway to Hancock, his father let him out of the carriage and pointed his son toward Hancock Academy. Then he turned the horse-driven carriage around, leaving Franklin to walk back to school in the pouring rain. Young Franklin Pierce quickly learned that actions speak louder than words. The event became a turning point in his life, a lesson he never forgot.

After Hancock Pierce went to Francestown Academy to prepare for college. While at Francestown, he stayed with friends of his father. He showed them great respect, but he was also known to pull pranks and roughhouse. Such behavior did not sit well with some of the "sober townspeople who boarded the schoolboys." Finally, in September 1820, he was ready to enter college.

Franklin attended Francestown Academy (right) to prepare for college.

——————— ✧

General Pierce preferred Bowdoin (pronounced bōhd-on) College in Brunswick, Maine, because its teachers favored the Democratic-Republican political ideals. By the time Franklin arrived at Bowdoin, he knew what his father expected of him. But he did not know how strict the college rules would be. Not even his father's unforgettable disciplinary lessons had prepared him for what would come next.

CHAPTER TWO

AWAY FROM HOME

If your past is limited, your future is boundless.
—Franklin Pierce, from his 1853 inaugural address

When Franklin Pierce entered Bowdoin College, he was, in his own words, "a very small slight and apparently frail boy of sixteen. My spirits were exuberant. I was far from my home without restraint except such as the government of a college imposed." And no one looked forward to his newfound freedom more than Franklin Pierce. Surely, he thought, there would be time for fun as well as learning. But the rules put on Bowdoin students quickly dampened his spirits.

Besides the required readings in Latin and Greek, students had to obey the *Laws of Bowdoin College*, a handbook for students. To Franklin the *Laws* read like a prison sentence: "No student shall eat or drink in any tavern unless in company with his parent . . . nor attend any theatrical entertainment or any idle show in Brunswick . . . nor play cards, billiards, or any game of hazard whatever for money . . . nor

In the *first year*, the English, Latin, and Greek languages, and Arithmetic; in the *second*, the several languages continued, together with Geography, Algebra,
Geometry, plane Trigonometry, Mensuration of Super-
ficies and Solids, Rhetoric, and Logic ;—in the *third*,
the several languages continued, together with Heights
and Distances, Gauging, Surveying, Navigation, Conic
Sections, Natural Philosophy, Chemistry, Metaphysics, History, and Theology ;—in the *fourth*, Chemistry, Metaphysics, and Theology continued, together
with Astronomy, Dialling, Spherical Geometry and
Trigonometry, with their application to astronomical
problems ; Ethics, Natural Law, and Civil Policy.
With these studies shall be intermixed frequent essays
in Elocution, English Composition, and Forensic Dis-
putation.

This page from the Laws of Bowdoin College *lists the classes that students were expected to take during each of their years in college.*

———————————— ✧ ————————————

go fishing . . . [nor] be concerned in loud and disorderly
singing . . . in shouting or clapping of hands, nor in
any . . . conduct [that is] dishonorable to the character of a
literary institution." And those who planned any visits or
"amusement" on Sundays courted suspension from college.

Nevertheless, Franklin and his friends found ways to get
around the strict rules. Beyond the campus, they found beautiful streams hidden amid the trees and wildflowers. They
spent many secret hours fishing there. They found small lakes
to swim in and hiding places to gather and talk freely. And

closer to town, they found a tavern. They knew it was forbidden territory, but it was too tempting to leave unexplored.

Such tastes of freedom cost Franklin plenty. His grades dropped. Though he was very popular among his friends— including future author Nathaniel Hawthorne—he was on the verge of failing. Eventually, he realized how badly his undisciplined lifestyle was affecting his studies. When he started his junior year at Bowdoin, he was determined to improve his dismal record, and he succeeded. By his senior year, he was chairman of the Athenaeans, one of the two literary societies at Bowdoin. He participated in debates, and he mastered his knowledge of science, politics, and religion.

"Science, politics, religion, friendship; in the midst of them the senior year wore away," biographer Nichols wrote, "and early in the summer the necessary preparations for commencement began to be made."

GRADUATING WITH PRIDE

By graduation day, Pierce had climbed from last place to fifth in his class. And Pierce spoke at the commencement ceremony on August 31, 1824. The ceremony ended with a message from Bowdoin College president William Allen to feel "a sacred thirst for truth . . . to seek knowledge rather than . . . gold."

For Franklin Pierce, friendships—lasting friendships—were even more important to him than all the studies he mastered at college. A poem by his friend Henry Wadsworth Longfellow expressed the gift of friendship that Pierce cherished:

How beautiful is youth! How bright its gleams
With its illusions, aspirations, dreams!

Book of beginnings, story without end,
Each maid a heroine, and each man a friend!

The class of 1824 had good reason to believe that their dreams of a happy and prosperous future would come true. The world was at peace. One year earlier, President James Monroe had issued the Monroe Doctrine. It formally declared

MONROE DOCTRINE

The Monroe Doctrine was named after James Monroe, who was elected president of the United States in 1816. At the time, the country was developing rapidly—adding new settlements in the western lands and building businesses in the North. To make sure that European countries would not try to set up colonies in the Western Hemisphere, he established the Monroe Doctrine. The doctrine, issued in 1823, during Monroe's second term in office, warned the European nations not to interfere in the governments of North and South America. The doctrine also stated that the United States would not interfere in the internal affairs of Europe and its existing colonies.

In 1823 Russia had established fur-trading settlements along the northwestern coast of North America. Also, many of Spain's colonies in Central and South America had recently declared their independence. Fear that Europe might help Spain retake its former colonies in the Americas drove President Monroe to issue the doctrine. Though he wrote the central parts of the work, his secretary of state, John Quincy Adams, outlined the details. And the Monroe Doctrine became a major part of U.S. foreign policy in the nineteenth century.

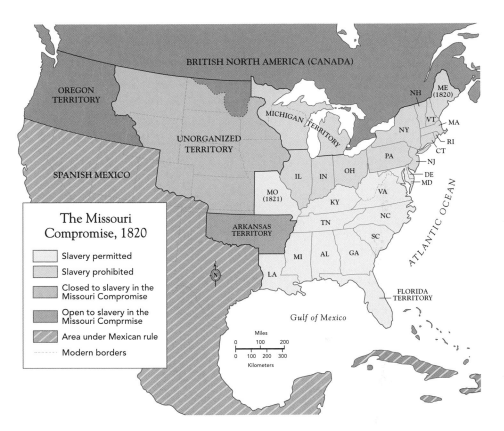

This map shows the areas of the United States that were slave states and free states at the time of the Compromise of 1820. Slavery was a divisive issue that could easily have torn the United States apart in the early 1800s.

——————————— ✦ ———————————

that the United States opposed any interference in North and South America by European countries. Meanwhile, under the Missouri Compromise, Maine had been admitted to the Union as a free state and Missouri as a slave state. This was done to keep a balance between free states and slave states. The compromise seemed to keep the disputed slavery issue quiet—at least for a while.

Farms were prospering. Roads to the western part of the country were opening up. And the nearly completed Erie Canal would join the waterways of the Great Lakes to the Atlantic Ocean. That offered new opportunities for manufactured goods and settlers to go westward. At the same

Erie Canal

After the War of 1812, a war against Great Britain at sea and Britain's colonies in Canada on land, the need for better transportation in the United States became clear. If supplies could have been sent by ship across northern New York, the war might have ended sooner. By 1816 building a waterway had become an important issue. New York residents dreamed of developing new businesses along a canal that would flow between Albany (on the Hudson River) and Buffalo (on Lake Erie). The route would also open up a whole new way to the western United States.

Finally, during the presidency of Martin Van Buren, the bill to construct the Erie Canal was passed. And in 1817, New York State authorized its construction, which lasted until 1825. For relief from their backbreaking work, workers put their aches and pains—and dreams—into songs. Singing together unified the workers and lifted their spirits.

The Erie Canal was 360 miles long, 40 feet wide, and 4 feet deep. It completely changed the freight business by delivering goods to more locations and at much lower costs. As railroads expanded, the canal competed by steadily enlarging. By 1909 the canal was big enough for barges and was the major part of the New York State Barge Canal System. The modern-day canal is 340 miles long, 150 feet wide, and 12 feet deep.

time, timber and farm products could be shipped eastward.

Franklin Pierce had no definite plans in mind for his future. But he was aware of the opportunities that awaited him. He was eager to explore them back home in Hillsborough. Pierce was sure of one thing: Like his father,

The Erie Canal in Lockport, New York, in the early 1830s. The lock shown at center raises or lowers a boat to the level of the canal in the direction it is going. The length of the Erie Canal in the 1830s changed in height a total of 568 feet and contained eighty-three locks.

he would serve his country by doing public service of some kind. And if a war should break out, he would welcome the chance to serve.

"KEEP MOVING!"

Following his father's advice to serve his country in peacetime as well as war, Pierce became postmaster in Hillsborough. He enjoyed serving the public. Like many college graduates, he also pursued a law degree. Gaining expertise in the field of law was important as the United States continued to expand. Land development and new business ventures required new rules and regulations. They also called for careful interpretation of existing laws. Historian Larry Gara recalled those early days in the country's history:

> *Wherever they settled, Americans took pride in their local communities. The location of a county seat, a canal, railroad, or military post seemed more important than national affairs.*
>
> *The federal government in Washington . . . was of little interest except when policies immediately affected local inhabitants.*

The United States of the early 1800s was an exciting place for an eager young man like Franklin Pierce. He seemed to already know that self-confidence would be the key to success. "There is nothing which so certainly establishes our prosperity as constant industry and a stern self-relying perseverance," he wrote, "and nothing surely contributes so much to our happiness as a fixed determination to be satisfied with the lot fortune has cast for us. You know my doctrine is that almost everything depends upon ourselves. We can be satisfied if we will."

But like his mother, Pierce grew discouraged at times. While in a sad mood, he wrote to his sister Betsey: "My prospects are Heaven knows what. . . . In every change that may be suggested to our minds, in almost every step we take there are a thousand considerations to be weighed." But he concluded that "in this funny old world" there is no way for one to improve oneself but to "push along" and "keep moving." Which is exactly what he did.

FROM LAW TO POLITICS

In Pierce's time, future lawyers prepared for their careers by working under practicing lawyers. Pierce spent a year in the law

office of John Burnham in Hillsborough. Then he moved across the state to Portsmouth. There, he spent the next two years in the law offices of Levi Woodbury. In 1827 he passed the bar exams. He was qualified to practice law in New Hampshire. Though law was his

✧ ────────────
Pierce worked for Levi Woodbury (left) for two years before passing the bar exam to become a lawyer.

profession, politics soon captured his attention.

The following year, 1828, Pierce joined rallies to support Andrew Jackson's candidacy for president. Jackson was a hero in the War of 1812. His soldiers called him Old Hickory because he was as tough as hickory wood. Jackson had also fought in the American Revolution when he was only thirteen years old. Such achievements fascinated Franklin Pierce.

All members of the Pierce family were fans of Andrew Jackson, who won the election. He became known as the People's President. Jackson pressed for the abolishment of the

————————————— ✧
Andrew Jackson (right) *believed in a strong presidency. During his presidency, he vetoed, or prevented from becoming law, more acts of Congress than the six presidents that came before him.*

Bank of the United States because it favored rich people and ignored the poor. And, under Jackson's leadership, the name of the Democratic-Republican Party was changed to the Democratic Party.

Pierce felt honored to be elected moderator of town meetings in New Hampshire. Town meetings helped to settle disputes between citizen groups. When he defeated his opponent, Dr. Samuel Hatch, for the post (the vote was 178–96), he seemed on his way up the political ladder. "So, the youthful lawyer with his ready smile and...ministerial manner, ascended the pulpit to preside over deliberations," biographer Nichols wrote. And Pierce's old college friend Nathaniel Hawthorne noted: "I remember meeting Pierce about this period, and catching from him some faint reflection of the zeal with which he was now stepping into the political arena."

Pierce gained more attention as speaker at a Jackson Day celebration. He was also appointed justice of the peace. And, to no one's surprise, Franklin Pierce was elected to the New Hampshire legislature in 1828. He served as a representative under a governor who happened to be his father. No longer was his future course unclear. He belonged in politics. And his goal was to serve the people who elected him.

Pierce was reelected to the legislature. In 1831, at the age of twenty-six, he became Speaker of the House. He was the youngest man ever to serve in that post. Pierce enjoyed the kind of popularity other politicians envied. The following year, he was elected to the U.S. Congress. With his father in the governor's office and Andrew Jackson in the White House, the world couldn't have looked brighter to this rising political star.

Washington, D.C., in 1833 when Pierce started his first session in the U.S. House of Representatives. Looking across the Potomac River, the White House is on the left and the U.S. Capitol is on the right.

CHAPTER THREE

TIME OUT FOR LOVE

The field of calm and free discussion in our country is open, and always will be so.
—Franklin Pierce, from his 1853 inaugural address

Before going to Washington, D.C., in 1833 for his first session in the U.S. House of Representatives, Pierce visited his sisters Betsey and Nancy in Boston. During his summer visit there, he became seriously ill with cholera, an intestinal disease. He recovered from the near-fatal illness in time to be sworn into office on December 2 in Washington. Like other congressmen at the time, Pierce stayed at a boardinghouse near the U.S. Capitol. (Few congressmen bought houses in Washington because the congressional sessions lasted only four months.) He enjoyed meeting other members of Congress who were also staying there. But his first impression of Washington, D.C., was not pleasant. He wrote to his father, "... there is too much roaring, swearing, lying and fawning to please decent folks."

No Women in the House

During Pierce's years in Congress, no women served in the House—the House of Representatives, that is. A congresswoman was unheard of in the mid-nineteenth century. Men dominated women in almost everything they did. They couldn't vote or go to college or get the same wages as men. Finally, in 1848, three hundred people gathered at Wesleyan Chapel in Seneca Falls, New York, for the first woman's rights convention in U.S. history.

At the convention, a small group of women led by Elizabeth Cady Stanton and Lucretia Coffin Mott wrote the *Declaration of Sentiments.* It proclaimed that all men *and*

✧ ————

Elizabeth Cady Stanton speaks to the first woman's rights convention in Seneca Falls, New York.

women are created equal. It also demanded that women be given the right to vote. Sixty-eight women and thirty-two men signed the historic document on July 20, 1848.

The document stated the facts concerning men's domination of women throughout the country's history:

> He has never permitted her to exercise her inalienable right to the elective franchise [vote]. He has compelled her to submit to laws, in the formation of which she had no voice.
>
> Having deprived her of . . . the elective franchise, thereby leaving her without representation in the halls of legislation, he has oppressed her on all sides. . . .
>
> He has denied her the facilities for obtaining a thorough education, all colleges being closed against her. . . .

Those are just a few of the facts listed in the *Declaration of Sentiments*. The *Declaration* launched the woman's rights movement in the United States. But it would take seventy-two years to bring about the Nineteenth Amendment to the Constitution that finally guaranteed a woman's right to vote.

Many of his colleagues were rough, hard-drinking men. Pierce knew it would be hard to hold their attention. It would be a challenge to win their votes on issues important to him. These issues included the Revolutionary War pensions bill, which would provide payment to Revolutionary War veterans. He supported veterans, but he vigorously opposed the bill. He feared fraud would occur due to lost records needed to verify claims. In his first speech before Congress in 1834, Pierce expressed his views on the topic. He received a warm response—especially, to his surprise, from southern members. Because of the South's growing bitterness toward the North over slavery, Pierce did not expect applause from his southern colleagues.

Pierce's popularity kept rising. He was appointed to the highly respected Judiciary Committee of the House of Representatives. His background in law served him well as he confronted a variety of legal matters. At the same time, he actively supported President Jackson's opposition to the Bank of the United States. He believed the bank was available only to rich customers. Like Jackson, Pierce favored a system of small banks. They would serve average Americans throughout the country. Pierce also remained loyal to the idea of more power to states and less to the federal government. Local projects, such as waterways, roads, and land management, should be decided mainly by the states in which they were located, he said.

OPPOSITES ATTRACT

Members of the Whig Party (later named the Republican Party) fought Jackson's policies. The Whigs supported a strong central banking system. They worked hard to defeat

Pierce's reelection, but they failed. Pierce was reelected in 1834. But one Whig Party supporter succeeded in winning the heart of Franklin Pierce. She was Jane Means Appleton from Amherst, New Hampshire. The exact time and place of their first meeting is unknown. They probably met through Jane's sister. She had married Alpheus Packard, one of Franklin's teachers at Bowdoin.

Jane came from a wealthy and prominent family. Her father, a former president of Bowdoin College, became a strong supporter of the Whigs. Jane grew up surrounded by fine art and music. She was a frail young woman. She suffered from

——————— ✧

Jane Pierce's father was Jesse Appleton (right) a well-known pastor and a former president of Bowdoin College. He died fifteen years before his daughter married Franklin Pierce.

tuberculosis, a lung disease, and had to watch her health carefully all of her life. She loved the quiet beauty of New Hampshire's countryside. Still, she would try to like Washington—if only to please Franklin.

The couple was married on November 19, 1834. The marriage took place in Amherst at the home of Jane's grandmother. The wedding was a small family gathering. The new bride and groom seemed to be opposites in every way except in their love for each other. Pierce was lively and sociable. He felt at home in taverns as well as halls of justice. Jane was shy, reclusive, and prone to illnesses.

——————— ✧
Jane Appleton Pierce

He grew up on a farm, in a large house that also served as a noisy tavern. She was raised in an atmosphere of quiet elegance. The couple seemed to prove the old saying that opposites attract each other.

Soon after their wedding, the Pierces left for Washington. There, they moved into a boardinghouse. Pierce appeared "well, in fine spirits, and apparently as happy as a man should be during the first month of the honeymoon," his friend Benjamin French noted. And in a letter to General Pierce, her father-in-law, Jane expressed her feelings at the time in her customary, formal way:

> We shall continue to be pleased with our accommodation here and are in fact as comfortably situated as we could be. . . . I find Washington very much as I expected both in appearance and climate—as to the former, my expectations were not very highly raised, and the latter has realized the favorable impression I had of it. . . . I have been out very frequently and intend to take your advice my dear sir, to exercise as much as possible in the open air.

CONFLICTING DREAMS

Jane's presence in Franklin's life made his work during Washington's dark winter months enjoyable. He wrote home, "I have been leading, I need not say, a very agreeable life—it has also been very quiet. . . . [Jane] is now enjoying better health." But Jane couldn't wait to return to New Hampshire in the spring. The busy life in Washington was beginning to affect her health and her moods.

When the Pierces returned home in March, they bought a house in Hillsborough. They spent the summer furnishing it, tending to it and to Pierce's law practice. Jane hoped that their peaceful way of life in New Hampshire would last forever. But in the fall of 1835, Pierce was reelected to Congress. Because of Jane's weak physical condition, she

SLAVERY

Slavery is a social system in which certain people own other people as private property. Slavery was practiced in ancient times throughout the world. In ancient Greece and Rome, captives from conquered lands served as a chief source of slaves. The first slaves in the American colonies arrived at Jamestown, the first British settlement in America, in 1620. At the time, African blacks were traded by the English, Spanish, and Portuguese and sold for work on plantations and in mines in America. By the early 1800s, most of Europe had abolished the slave trade. But slavery still flourished in the United States—on southern plantations in particular, where slaves harvested crops from dawn until dusk. They earned nothing, but their owners became rich from the sale of the crops.

The abolition movement—led by such people as William Lloyd Garrison and Frederick Douglass—worked to abolish (end) slavery in the South. The slavery issue divided the North, which opposed slavery, and the South, where slavery was big business. To avoid a bloody civil war, President Pierce tried to satisfy demands of both the North and South. But he failed to see the immorality of slavery itself. The Civil War (1861–1865) erupted four years after Pierce left office. In 1863 Abraham Lincoln's

decided to stay with relatives in Boston. Franklin stayed in Washington to work.

In 1835 Congress faced two important issues. One was the question of slavery. According to law, slaves were the property of white slave owners—something they owned. Slaves had no rights. Laws were in place to give slave owners

Many southerners fought to keep slavery because it enabled their way of life. Slaves were cheap labor for picking cotton on plantations such as this one on the Mississippi River.

Emancipation Proclamation declared that all slaves in territories under Southern control were free. Later, slavery was outlawed by the Thirteenth Amendment, ratified in late 1865.

the right to recapture fugitive (escaped) slaves. People caught helping slaves escape would be severely fined or punished. The other issue dealt with tariffs. Tariffs are taxes a government puts on goods brought into or shipped out of the country. Franklin looked forward to debating these issues. He also planned to defend states' rights. From his point of view, each state had the right to make its own decisions, including the right to decide the slavery issue, without interference from the federal government. All the while, however, he worried about Jane's health and her happiness.

CHAPTER FOUR

FROM JOY TO SORROW

We have nothing in our history . . .
to invite aggression: we have
everything to beckon us to peace.
—Franklin Pierce, from his 1853 inaugural address

Pierce's friend James Polk was Speaker of the House in 1835. Both men were fierce defenders of states' rights. Pierce expressed his strong views during the growing debate on slavery in the United States. The topic was driving a wedge between the North, which wanted to free the slaves, and the South, which relied on slave labor. Personally, Pierce did not approve of slavery. His family had never owned slaves. But he didn't want to risk the withdrawal of the southern states from the Union. Because of this view, he did not oppose the right of those states to practice slavery. He stuck to his firm belief that states had the right to decide the slavery issue for themselves—without interference from the federal government. He was so firm in his

James Polk (right) was a slave owner who thought slavery was immoral. He freed his slaves after the death of his wife and thought slavery would eventually die out on its own.

———————— ✧

support of states' rights—guaranteed by the Constitution— that he failed to see slavery as a moral issue. Holding the states together and avoiding civil war was more important to Pierce than ending slavery. But the abolitionists (those who were devoted to freeing the slaves) were determined to abolish the inhuman practice of slavery—even if it took a war to do so.

During that same session, Senator John C. Calhoun verbally attacked Pierce. Calhoun claimed that Pierce had falsified the number of New Hampshire residents favoring abolition. Pierce countered the attack by claiming he had been misquoted. Pierce won. But Calhoun's unfair accusation took a toll on Pierce's health.

Also, some of Pierce's friends liked to party and drink too much. They began to lure him into doing the same.

His Whig opponents were quick to label him a drunkard. They publicized this as fact. Pierce quickly learned the importance of drinking in moderation to avoid attracting negative public attention.

While tackling disputes in Congress, Pierce received joyous news from home. The Pierce's first child, Franklin Jr., was born on February 2, 1836. But the joy quickly turned to sorrow. The baby died just three days after his birth. Nothing could have saddened his parents more. Jane became deeply depressed. Franklin, exhausted from his congressional work, came down with pleurisy, a disease that affects the lungs. Grief, depression, and physical illness troubled both Pierce and his wife.

GROWING BATTLES

When Pierce recovered, he returned to Congress in March 1836. He found still greater political battles waiting there. Texas had won its independence from Mexico. It would become a state. But would Texas join the Union as a slave state or a free state? The spread of slavery ignited more heated debate about the slavery issue than ever before. On behalf of citizens throughout the country, abolitionists sent petitions to Congress demanding an end to the spread of slavery.

But the House of Representatives issued a "gag resolution." This was a rule that prevented members of Congress from even discussing the petitions.

Then bills to admit Michigan and Arkansas to the Union were introduced in Congress. More debate and disorder followed those bills. "A rough and tumble fight in the press gallery enlivened the situation," Professor Nichols

In the nineteenth century, arguments in Congress (left) sometimes became heated and even violent.

✧ ————————

noted. After a five-day debate, delayed by the drunken be-havior of some members, Congress passed the bills to admit the two new states.

A decision about the recognition of Texas as a state was put on hold. Pierce approved of the delay. He was still cop-ing with his illness and grief. He would do anything to avoid more turmoil in Congress. When the 1836 session came to an end, Pierce was happy to go home. When he arrived in New Hampshire, he found that his popularity was still widespread. In fact he was so popular that he was elected a U.S. senator from his beloved state.

Pierce returned to Washington in March 1837. He was thrilled that Jane could join him. Though she still battled depression, she wanted to support her husband in his first term in the Senate. They moved into a new boardinghouse owned by Mrs. C. A. Pittman. Unlike other boarding-houses, Mrs. Pittman's did not allow wine to be served. "There is not a wine drinker among us," a boarder wrote. "Even Franklin Pierce has left off."

CALM UNDER PRESSURE

Pierce served on the Judiciary Committee. But his work on the committee to investigate the banking industry took up most of his time. Again, his personal life clouded his work in Congress. His father suffered a stroke. His sister Harriet

————————————— ✦

Franklin Pierce's public life went smoothly, but his private life endured many hardships.

suffered an unknown illness. And Jane felt weak most of the winter. Still, Pierce did his best to represent his state. He was the youngest senator in Washington. He was surrounded by great public speakers, such as Henry Clay, Daniel Webster, and John Calhoun. Pierce participated on several different committees, but he was not responsible for any major legislation or policy. He spent most of his time in committee rooms where he faithfully performed many assignments. He worked to oppose the abolitionists and to defend his stand on states' rights. The abolitionists, however, were growing in strength and number.

Jane Pierce longed to leave Washington. She wanted to get away from the noise and activity of the city. "Oh, how I wish he [Franklin] was out of political life!" she wrote. "How much better it would be on every account!" But

Clay (left), *Calhoun* (center), *and Webster* (right) *were just a few of the notable senators who served at the same time as Pierce.*

Pierce continued to serve his country and his party as a senator. After all, he had promised to do so. He voted against projects that required federal funds. He even opposed the Alabama, Florida, and Georgia Railroad. He did, however, vote for the completion of roads in Michigan. That project had been started before the territory became a state. And his was the deciding vote when the bill passed. He voted for it because he believed that projects already started should be completed. And he continued to speak out for the right of each state to decide the slavery issue for itself.

When the session ended, the Pierces returned to New Hampshire. They decided to move from Hillsborough to Concord. Greater opportunities for Franklin's law practice existed in Concord—once his term in the Senate was over. Just thinking about the future made Jane Pierce feel better.

Franklin Pierce's political career was advancing quickly in 1839.

CHAPTER FIVE

LOOKING FORWARD

*You have a right . . . to expect your
agents in every department to regard
strictly the limits imposed on them by the
Constitution of the United States.*
—Franklin Pierce, from his 1853 inaugural address

In 1839 the Pierces' second child, Franklin Robert (Franky), was born. The new baby helped to fill the void created after Franklin Jr.'s death. But joy continued to mix with sorrow. Pierce's father died that same year, following his mother's death the year before. Yet Pierce's popularity in both Washington and New Hampshire warmed his heart. By 1840 his reputation as a great public speaker and campaigner was secure. He was in constant demand to help Democrats win elections. Pierce attended a rousing meeting in Sullivan County to rally Democratic spirit. Afterward, Pierce wrote, "It was a glorious meeting and enlivened a spirit in Sullivan County." He did the same in Massachusetts. And when

Pierce helped Martin Van Buren (left) win votes in New Hampshire.

✧ ————————————————

President Martin Van Buren ran for reelection in 1841, Pierce campaigned for him "with frankness, candor and fervid eloquence."

Pierce was proud that Van Buren carried New Hampshire with six thousand votes. That was the largest vote ever polled there up to that time. Yet Van Buren lost the election. And the Democrats lost power in Congress to the Whigs. Pierce had always been a part of the political party that had the majority in Congress. But in 1841, the Democrats became the minority party. The Whigs had won more seats in Congress as well as the presidency. But soon there was good news too.

On April 13, 1841, Jane gave birth to another son, Benjamin (Bennie). He was named after his grandfather. Franklin was overjoyed with his growing family.

In the Senate, Pierce worked hard. He spent much of his time making sure that remaining Revolutionary War veterans received proper benefits, such as medical care, in their retirement. The veterans' welfare had special meaning to him. His father had served heroically in that war.

During his last two sessions in the Senate, Pierce paid more attention to his health. "He undertook the strict requirements which he had prescribed for himself in previous winters. He had plenty of exercise, gave up alcohol and tobacco," Nichols noted. Yet he was exhausted. Jane urged him to retire.

Finally, on February 16, 1842, her dream came true. Pierce resigned from the Senate. Like Jane, he looked forward to returning—permanently—to New Hampshire. He wanted a closer family life with his wife and two young sons. The children seemed to make him feel younger. They gave him a new purpose in life.

A PEACEFUL EXIT

Pierce's colleagues regretted his leaving the Senate, because he had been a hard worker. He also showed absolute loyalty to the Democratic Party. But some thought he was too eager to satisfy the South by accepting slavery for the sake of unity. They claimed he ignored the issue by leaving the slavery decision for states to solve. Throughout his term in the Senate, Pierce had tried to keep the lid on the potentially explosive issue.

On February 26, 1842, Pierce, Jane, three-year-old Franky, and Bennie moved into their house in Concord. Retirement from the Senate allowed Pierce time to concentrate on building his law practice. Like many Americans, he had lost money in the economic depression of 1837. Prices had gone up while the value of paper money went down. He looked forward to making up his losses. And because of his continued popularity, he hoped to help local Democrats seeking office. It didn't take long for requests to come in.

As Concord's best-known lawyer, Pierce succeeded in prosecuting those who sold liquor without a license to do so. Soon members of the temperance society asked him to speak at town meetings. He spoke in support of their goal—to end the consumption of alcohol in Concord. They believed that crime and poverty were caused by the use of alcohol. They hoped that Concord, like its neighboring towns, would become "dry"—free of alcohol.

Pierce's former opponents in the Whig Party publicly joked about his involvement in the temperance cause. They recalled his social drinking in Washington and called him a hypocrite. They wanted liquor to be sold openly in Concord without needing a license to do so. Political candidates began to take sides. Pierce stood by the local Democrats, and together they won. Concord became a dry town.

During Pierce's involvement in town meetings, his two sons became ill with typhus. Bacteria spread by lice and other tiny organisms cause this disease. Bennie recovered, but on November 14, 1843, Franky died. He was only four years old. Jane Pierce was overcome with sorrow. Franklin was stunned. "In all my labors, plans and exertions in them [the children] was the center of all my hopes," he wrote. The Pierces had these words inscribed on Franky's grave: "A loved and precious treasure lost to us here but safe in the Redeemer's care."

LIVING WITH TRAGEDY

Pierce tried to overcome the tragic loss by keeping active in local events. Jane Pierce dealt with her depression by seek-

Jane Pierce (right) *clung to her son Bennie after the death of her son Franky.*

ing privacy and staying close to Bennie. Pierce adored the boy, who became the light of his life. Soon he would be telling the same Revolutionary War stories to Bennie that General Pierce had told him.

But the war that began to affect Pierce in 1844 was the political war between the Whigs and the Democrats. Democrats wanted to regain power in Congress and the White House. When Pierce learned that his old friend James Polk would be the Democratic Party's nominee in the upcoming presidential election, he was thrilled.

Like Pierce, Polk believed that any decision about slavery should be made by the states—not the federal government. Like Pierce, Polk wanted the government to remain free from responsibility for the slavery issue. Both insisted that the people's right to own slaves was supported by the

Pierce's friend James Polk (left) won the 1844 presidential election.

✧ ————————————

Constitution. But was slavery moral? Was it moral to buy and sell people? The abolitionists said no. It was the morality of the issue—not the politics—that concerned them. The issue haunted the Democrats. They voted to allow slavery in states that approved it.

With Pierce's help, Polk won New Hampshire. He also won the election, becoming the eleventh president of the United States in 1845. Polk offered Pierce the post of attorney general. Pierce turned it down, however. His main concern was still his family—not political office. And his law practice was thriving. "His winsome ways and likable personality helped Pierce as a trial lawyer to bring juries to his point of view," historian Larry Gara wrote. But New Hampshire Democrats would never stop trying to lure Pierce back into national politics.

GENERAL FRANKLIN PIERCE

Pierce continued to turn down political opportunities—
including a request to return to the U.S. Senate. Then a
chance to serve his country in a war came along. He couldn't
resist it. Since childhood, he had wanted to be a war hero
like his father—or at least try to be one.

The war with Mexico began in 1846. The previous year,
Texas had become a state that allowed slavery. The United
States wanted to extend the new state's border to the Rio
Grande. At the same time, the United States wanted to
carve the states of New Mexico and California out of
Mexican territory. Shortly after enlisting as a private in the
U.S. Army, Pierce received a promotion to colonel.

Jane Pierce did not want her husband to enlist. Still, she
knew the importance of his fulfilling a lifelong dream.

───────────── ✧ ─────────────

*This map shows the area of dispute between Texas and
Mexico that started the Mexican War (1846–1848).*

Pierce was a brigadier
general in the U.S. Army
during the Mexican War.

✧ ─────────────

When he became a brigadier general, that dream became a
reality. He led a brigade in an attack on Churubusco on
August 20, 1847. The battles of Churubusco and Contreras
were some of the main battles of the Mexican War.

Biographer Rubel described the turning point event of
Pierce's service on the battlefield:

> He saw his first action in August 1847 at
> Contreras, where poorly aimed but quite noisy

artillery fire caused his horse to jump. This pressed Pierce's groin fiercely against the high pommel of his saddle, causing temporary (but nevertheless excruciating) pain. The general passed out.

Pierce suffered injuries to his neck and head. Later, he became ill with dysentery (a severe intestinal disorder). But General Winfield Scott praised his service. On September 12, U.S. troops took Mexico City, the Mexican capital. Pierce had a strong devotion to duty. He was eager to help others. Because of these traits, he won praise from his soldiers and fellow officers. Yet he was disappointed not to have served as heroically as his father had. Having fulfilled his wartime service, he was ready to give up public service and return home to New Hampshire.

Pierce (on the horse facing the water) *and his troops land in Mexico.*

New States and Tighter Laws

As a result of the Mexican War, the United States acquired much of the territory that makes up the southwestern part of the country. In 1846 it also acquired the Oregon Territory from Great Britain. More than 32 million people lived in the United States at the time. More people were coming from all over the world to live in a democratic country. Gold and other metals attracted miners and prospectors. Cotton fields attracted future landowners. But the production of cotton depended on unpaid slaves. The slaves were given plain food, clothing, and housing in shacks on their owners' property in return for their backbreaking work and nothing more.

Fugitive slave laws protected slave owners. When runaway slaves were caught, they were imprisoned and returned to their owners or killed. Those helping slaves to escape to the North—and to freedom—were heavily fined or imprisoned.

This print shows white men hunting four black men. Fugitive slave laws allowed whites to treat all blacks as possible fugitive slaves. Some free blacks became slaves because of these laws.

FINDING PEACE AMID TURMOIL

In 1848 voters elected Zachary Taylor the twelfth president of the United States. He was a Whig and a Mexican War hero. Two years later, Henry Clay, Pierce's former foe in the Senate, drafted the Compromise of 1850. It tightened the existing fugitive slave laws. The compromise also allowed California to become a free state. The compromise banned slave trade in the capital, Washington, D.C. And the territories of Utah and New Mexico became states with nothing said about slavery. Franklin Pierce supported the compromise. He thought it would help keep order and avoid turmoil.

The South was satisfied because the compromise stiffened the punishment of fugitive slaves and their helpers. It also gave slave owners the right to recapture their slaves. Making

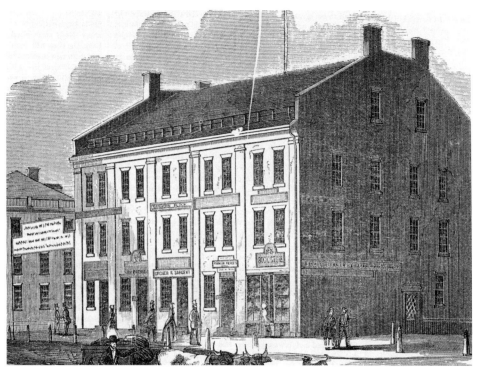

*Pierce used the second shop from the right in this building
for his law office in Concord, New Hampshire.*

──────────────── ✧ ────────────────

California a nonslave state and ending slave trade in
Washington satisfied the North temporarily. But the Whigs
and the Democrats remained divided on the slavery issue.

Franklin Pierce was relieved to be living peacefully in
the hills of New Hampshire. He liked being far away from
the heated debates in Congress. The Mexican War was behind him. His growing law practice was ahead of him. He
was content to be free of the frenzy of national politics.

Both political parties held conventions in 1852 to nominate a candidate for president for the November election.

Pierce was not surprised to learn that the Whigs had nom-
inated General Winfield Scott at their convention. He was
another Mexican War hero. A war hero would be hard to
beat. Pierce offered to help by rallying support in New
Hampshire for the Democratic nominee to be chosen at the
Democratic convention in June. The leading contenders for
the party's nomination included Lewis Cass of Michigan,
James Buchanan of Pennsylvania, William L. Marcy of New
York, Samuel Houston of Texas, Stephen A. Douglas of
Illinois, and Thomas Benton of Missouri. All were well
qualified. Convention delegates would have to unite behind
one of them. But would they? Could they?

*Pierce was not well known in politics outside of his home state of
New Hampshire, but many people there wanted him to be
one of the Democratic candidates for president in 1852.*

CHAPTER SIX

"WHO'S FRANKLIN PIERCE?"

You have summoned me in my weakness;
you must sustain me by your strength.
—Franklin Pierce, from his 1853 inaugural address

On June 1, 1852, six hundred delegates met at the Democratic National Convention in Baltimore, Maryland. They had to choose their nominee for president. All the candidates in the race were well known and respected. Still, New Hampshire citizens were not satisfied with the list. They wanted their favorite Democrat—Franklin Pierce—to enter the race. He said no. But his old friend and former congressman Edmund Burke refused to give up on Pierce. He pleaded with Pierce to let his name be added to the list of contenders. He told Pierce he would not have to campaign. He could stay in New Hampshire. And he was unknown to most of the delegates, so his name probably would not be recognized on the list. Yet, people in his home state hoped to see it there.

Pierce finally agreed to have his name introduced at the convention—but only as a last resort and only if no other candidate could win a majority of votes. That, Pierce thought, would never happen. He assured his wife that entering his name would please his fellow citizens who had been so loyal to him. And his name was almost totally unknown outside of New Hampshire. Chances were highly unlikely that it would even be mentioned.

On June 4, the last day of the convention, delegates stayed up all night trying to decide on a nominee. Everyone on the list of leading contenders had campaigned to win. Chairman John W. Davis urged the delegates to "cultivate harmony" for the sake of the party. Yet, after many ballots were taken, they could not agree on a nominee. The con-

The 1852 Democratic National Convention took place in Baltimore, Maryland (above). In 1850 Baltimore was the second-largest city in the United States.

vention was deadlocked. As a last resort, Pierce's name was called. And many asked, "Who's Franklin Pierce?"

But the little they knew about Pierce was positive. He had been loyal to the Democratic Party. He had served his country well. He was popular in the North and had favored the Compromise of 1850. That was enough to unite the candidates. On the forty-ninth ballot, Pierce became the party's nominee for president.

SHOCKING NEWS

During the convention in Baltimore, Franklin and Jane Pierce were enjoying a leisurely trip in their carriage to visit friends in Boston. On the way, they dropped Bennie off in Andover to visit family friends there. As the Pierces went on to Boston, a friend stopped their carriage. He told them the news of Pierce's nomination. Pierce was stunned. Jane fainted. "Mrs. Pierce could not stand it; this result was too dreadful," biographer Nichols wrote. Later, Bennie wrote to his mother, "I hope he won't be elected, for I should not like to live in Washington and I know you would not either."

Back in Concord, the people were thrilled. Nichols described the joyous mood there:

> New Hampshire's capital had enjoyed a most un-
> usual state of excitement ever since . . . the news
> came. Concord for the space of the next eight
> months was to be the heart of the political
> world. . . . During the last few days, Main Street
> had been one continuous political meeting.
> . . . Now that the [brigadier] general had re-
> turned, the whole town thronged to extend their

congratulations. Wednesday evening the Concord brass band serenaded him, and in answer [he spoke to them] in a happy and complimentary manner.

Supporters quickly wrote biographies to inform the country about Franklin Pierce. Nathaniel Hawthorne was one of the most famous writers in the United States. He wrote about Pierce's belief in states' rights regarding slavery. He believed Pierce's view was in agreement with the Constitution. He saw in Pierce "evidences of patriotism, integrity, and courage." He concluded "that he had in him many of the chief elements of a great ruler." Hawthorne

✧ ————————————
Nathaniel Hawthorne
(left) *had written and published many books by 1852, including his best known novel,*
The Scarlet Letter.

had always been loyal to Pierce. He simply wrote what he
believed. But the *New York Times* claimed that Hawthorne's
book about Pierce was an "extremely biased political tract
intended solely for electioneering effect."

The Whig Party was unorganized. Nevertheless, it did its
best to attack Pierce during the campaign. They reminded
voters that Pierce had fainted during the Mexican War. They
labeled him a do-nothing in Congress. And they joked
about his drinking while in Washington. Democrats, in
turn, made charges against General Scott, the Whig candidate. They labeled him anti-Catholic, "pompous, and argu-
mentative." They nicknamed him Old Fuss and Feathers.

──────────────── ✧ ────────────────

*A political cartoon from 1852 shows the Whig candidate,
Winfield Scott (left), pulling the "Presidential Chair" out
from under Democratic candidate Franklin Pierce.*

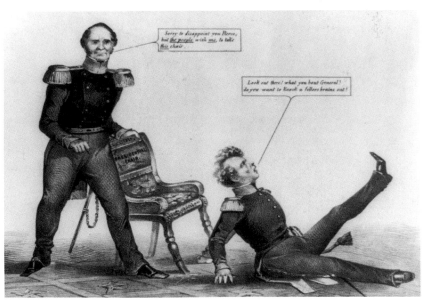

*An 1852 campaign poster shows Pierce (left)
and his running mate, William R. King of Alabama.*

The Free-Soil and the Liberty parties, groups that opposed slavery in the United States, had split off from the mainstream parties. They supported their own candidates. But thanks to Hawthorne's writings and unified Democratic Party publicity, Pierce provided strong competition for General Scott.

On election day, Pierce attended the funeral of U.S. statesman Daniel Webster in Boston. "By eleven that evening, as the votes were counted, Pierce realized that he was to be the next president of the United States," Nichols noted. "He allowed no demonstration and [the] next morning he went back to the land of hills where at his sacred places, his birthplace, his old familiar haunts, his father's grave, he sought to take courage for his overwhelming task."

Pierce (above) won the 1852 election by fewer than 215,000 votes.

CHAPTER SEVEN

BITTERSWEET VICTORY

I acknowledge my obligations to the masses of my countrymen, and to them alone.

—Franklin Pierce, from his 1853 inaugural address

The presidential election of 1852 was a close one. Pierce won 1,601,474 votes and Scott won 1,386,580. The Free-Soil candidate, John P. Hale, won 156,667 votes. Free-Soilers had been gaining more and more followers as fugitive slave laws grew stricter. The Free-Soil Party insisted on stopping the spread of slavery into new states. The much smaller Liberty Party wanted to end slavery everywhere in the United States. The election showed how divided the country was becoming. And Pierce's states' rights view of slavery had already begun to weaken his popularity in the North. Could he hold the country together? Or would the antislavery groups divide it? That was the question and the burden Pierce faced as Inauguration Day approached.

Between the election in November 1852 and the inauguration in March 1853, Pierce focused on choosing his cabinet. The cabinet is the president's group of chief advisers. Careful consideration of each proposed member took time and patience. To relieve the pressure of preinauguration days, the Pierces enjoyed visiting friends and relatives in Massachusetts. After one particular visit on January 6, 1853, Franklin, Jane, and Bennie boarded a train in Boston for their return to Concord. Pierce was anxious to get home and prepare for his family's move to Washington two months later. Then tragedy struck. Less than a mile from the Concord station, an accident occurred. Bennie was crushed to death in the train wreckage. Pierce and his wife were not hurt.

This illustration from the January 22, 1853, edition of the Concord Illustrated News *shows the accident that killed Pierce's son, Bennie. Their car detached from the train and fell down a rocky ledge.*

Bennie's death was almost too much for his mother to bear. She did not appear in public for months. Pierce was devastated by the loss of his beloved son. But he still had to choose his cabinet and write his inaugural address. Many wondered how he could carry on with his duties after such a great personal tragedy. He had lost all of his children, whom he had called the "center of all my hopes."

LIKE FATHER, LIKE SON

But Pierce had been called to serve his country. Like his father, he wouldn't hesitate to respond. On Inauguration Day, March 4, 1853, the Congress, the Supreme Court, and various diplomats gathered in the Senate chamber. There, Chief Justice Roger B. Taney administered the oath of office to Franklin Pierce. At forty-eight years old, Pierce was the country's youngest president up to that time.

Pierce (center, facing left) *takes the presidential oath of office in front of a large crowd at the U.S. Capitol on March 4, 1853.*

FREEDOM OF EXPRESSION

Great American writers flourished while Pierce was president. They included his good friends Nathaniel Hawthorne and Henry Wadsworth Longfellow. Other famous authors were Herman Melville, Ralph Waldo Emerson, John Whittier, Emily Dickinson, Henry David Thoreau, Walt Whitman, and Harriet Beecher Stowe.

Thoreau's *Walden, or Life in the Woods* awakened readers to the simple pleasures and lessons learned while living alone in the woods near Walden Pond in Massachusetts. In *Walden*, he warned busy Americans: "Our life is frittered away by detail. . . . Simplify, simplify." He wrote, "If a man does not keep pace with his companions, perhaps it is because he hears a different drummer. Let him step to the music which he hears, however measured or far away."

Publishers refused to print Walt Whitman's now-famous *Leaves of Grass*, because they thought his style was too free and open and the subject matter—ordinary people doing ordinary tasks—too revolutionary. Whitman wanted to depart from the lofty topics of earlier poets and to celebrate the common people instead. He finally published the work himself, and he dedicated it to the "brave" as well as the "cowardly," to both the "spiritual and sweating humanity."

Poetry that celebrated ordinary human beings in all aspects of real life and that used everyday language to do so stunned mid-nineteenth century critics and colleagues alike. John Whittier burned the book! But Emerson praised Whitman for his "free and brave thought." And he added, "I greet you at the beginning of a great career." But Whitman's greatness was not realized until after his death. In modern times, his celebrations of freedom and equality are read in classrooms everywhere.

I celebrate myself, and sing myself,
And what I assume you shall assume,

The title page of Harriet Beecher Stowe's
Uncle Tom's Cabin
─────────────── ✧

UNCLE TOM'S CABIN;

OR,

LIFE AMONG THE LOWLY.

BY

HARRIET BEECHER STOWE.

VOL. I.

ONE HUNDRED AND FIFTH THOUSAND.

BOSTON:
JOHN P. JEWETT & COMPANY
CLEVELAND, OHIO:
JEWETT, PROCTOR & WORTHINGTON.
1852.

For every atom belonging to
me as good belongs to you. . . .

But it was Harriet Beecher Stowe's
novel, *Uncle Tom's Cabin*, that sent
shock-waves throughout the South.
The antislavery story was published in
1852, and it boosted the abolition
movement. Its stark truth about the
horrors of slavery aroused sympathy
for slaves and awakened the world to
the tyranny of the system. The book
became an international best-seller, and Ralph Waldo
Emerson's review tells us why:

> *We have seen an American woman write a novel
> of which a million copies were sold in all
> languages, and which had one merit, of speaking
> to the universal heart, and was read with equal
> interest to three audiences, namely, in the parlor,
> in the kitchen, and in the nursery of every house.*

Writers such as Thoreau, Whitman, and Stowe opened the
doors to greater freedom of expression in American literature.
In writing about the experiences and feelings of ordinary
people, they touched the hearts of readers.

Pierce delivered his inaugural address—3,319 words—completely from memory. He used no manuscript, no notes. The opening line of the speech revealed the anguish he felt on that historic day:

> It is a relief to feel that no heart but my own can know the personal regret and bitter sorrow over which I have been borne to a position so suitable for others rather than desirable for myself.

Later in the speech, Pierce expressed his hope that the slavery question was "at rest" and "that no sectional or fanatical excitement may again threaten the disability of our institutions or obscure the light of our prosperity."

The audience cheered, but across the country the anti-slavery movement was far from "at rest." Pierce had neither the energy nor the passion to deal with a divided country. Professor Gara noted, "Whether he was capable of providing creative leadership at a time of change in so many areas of American life remained to be seen."

THE TENANT FOR A TIME

President Pierce chose his cabinet members wisely. They came from various states and worked well together. Pierce's vice president, William King, had been ill for some time and died on April 19. Pierce never replaced him. A few weeks later, President and Mrs. Pierce settled down in the White House. Because Jane Pierce was still overwhelmed with grief over Bennie's death, she stayed in their private quarters. She asked her old friend and distant relative Abby A. Means to act as official hostess at White House events.

Pierce chose his cabinet members carefully. They were Secretary of State William L. Marcy (center), and (clockwise from top) Secretary of the Navy James C. Dobbin, Secretary of War Jefferson Davis, Postmaster General James Campbell, Secretary of the Treasury James Guthrie, Secretary of the Interior Robert McClelland, and Attorney General Caleb Cushing.

President Pierce liked to go out and meet people whenever he could. He often walked alone on the streets outside the White House.

Once he told some passersby, "You need no introduction to this house, it is your house and I am but the tenant for a time." Sometimes he was seen riding horseback around Washington, as he visited friends. Except for one time when a drunk man threw a hard-boiled egg at him, he roamed about Washington freely without incident. (The egg thrower was arrested, but Pierce never pressed charges.)

*Jane Pierce's grief over the loss of her son put a
somber mood over the whole White House* (above).

———————————————— ◇ ————————————————

Eventually, Jane Pierce began to attend some public
functions—but only out of a sense of duty. Her thoughts
were still of her son. She even wrote letters to the dead boy.
One visitor commented on the sorrow that seemed to fill
the White House. "Everything in that mansion seems cold
and cheerless. I have seen hundreds of log cabins which
seemed to contain more happiness." Yet the private quarters were usually filled with relatives who helped to lift
Jane's spirits.

SETTING BOUNDARIES

Free time became harder and harder for Pierce to find.
Both national and world problems demanded his attention.
The Treaty of Guadalupe Hidalgo had ended the Mexican

War. But it had not clearly marked the boundary between Mexico and the United States. In May, Pierce sent James Gadsden, his minister to Mexico, to settle the boundary disputes. The land was important to the United States. It created the most convenient route for a transcontinental railroad to reach the Pacific coast across the South. For ten million dollars Gadsden bought almost thirty thousand square miles of territory south of the Gila River. The land later became southern Arizona and southern New Mexico.

The historic transfer of land was called the Gadsden Purchase. It was named after the skillful diplomat who

———————————————— ✧ ————————————————

This map shows the territories of Texas and California and the Gadsden Purchase that was made in 1853 during Pierce's presidency.

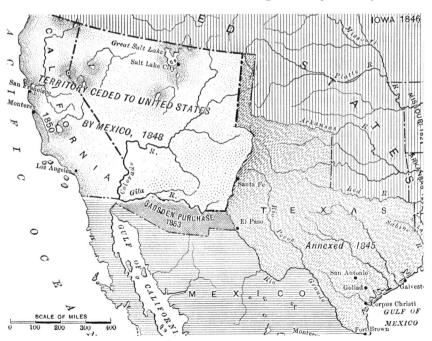

acquired the land. The transfer was officially approved by both countries on December 30, 1853. The purchase marked the end of U.S. expansion. For the first time, map-makers outlined the continental United States, which has remained unchanged.

Midwesterners wanted a railroad to pass through their area too. They knew that such direct transportation would attract more people and spur business growth. Senator Stephen Douglas of Illinois had money invested in rail-roads. He needed support from Congress to pass a railroad bill for the Midwest. To win votes from his southern col-leagues, he proposed to let the territories of Kansas and Nebraska choose whether they wanted to be free or slave states. Douglas's proposal led to the Kansas-Nebraska Act.

✧ ————————

Stephen Douglas proposed the Kansas-Nebraska Act, allowing Kansas and Nebraska to vote on becoming slave or free states.

FAILED COMPROMISES

The Missouri Compromise of 1820 allowed Missouri to join the Union as a slave state and Maine as a free (nonslave) state. Henry Clay, Speaker of the House of Representatives at the time, worked hard to pass the laws, which were created to bring an even balance in Congress. But balance was not easily maintained. Disputes continued to develop between proslavery and antislavery groups.

By the 1850s, the disputes had turned into violent debates. Once again, Henry Clay led members of Congress to pass new laws to combat the increasing turmoil around the slavery issue. He drafted the Compromise of 1850, which allowed each state to decide whether or not to allow slavery within its borders. The compromise admitted California to the Union as a slave-free state and admitted the territories of Utah and New Mexico with no mention of slavery. The compromise banned slavery in Washington, D.C.

The Kansas-Nebraska Act of 1854 brought up the matter again. Under it, the territories of Kansas and Nebraska (modern Kansas, Colorado, Nebraska, Wyoming, Montana, and parts of North Dakota and South Dakota) would be allowed to choose their position on slavery.

But these compromises failed to deal with the inhumanity of the slave trade. They were temporary solutions that pushed off the eventual conflict that became the Civil War.

The act overturned the Missouri Compromise of 1820. It extended slavery farther north, beyond the boundary previously agreed upon.

To satisfy his colleagues from the North, Douglas explained that he was not ignoring the Missouri Compromise of 1820. Instead, he said he was complying with the Compromise of 1850. That legislation clearly allowed the slavery issue to be decided by the citizens themselves. But to get his bill passed, Douglas needed President Pierce's support. Both Douglas and southern politician Jefferson Davis warned Pierce that if he refused to support the

———————————— ✧ ————————————

This political cartoon shows Pierce (kneeling left) helping other Democratic political figures force slavery down the throat of a Free-Soiler. The Free-Soil Party opposed the spread of slavery and blamed the Democratic Party for the Kansas-Nebraska Act, which allowed slavery to spread.

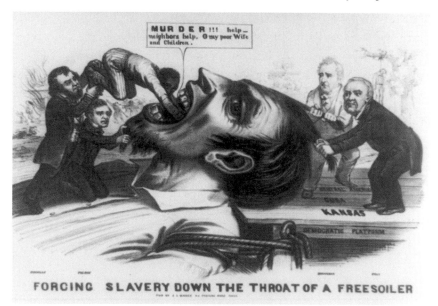

FORCING SLAVERY DOWN THE THROAT OF A FREESOILER

Kansas-Nebraska Act, Congress might disallow the Gadsden Purchase. Cornered and afraid of creating more bitterness within the parties, Pierce agreed to sign it. He seemed to have no choice but to support the Kansas-Nebraska Act of 1854. The bill passed by a narrow margin in both houses of Congress.

MOUNTING OPPOSITION

Almost immediately after Pierce signed the bill, brutal battles broke out in Kansas. The abolitionist Jayhawkers battled the Border Ruffians, a proslavery faction from Missouri. Fearful of more threats from southern senators, Pierce sided with the proslavery groups. The stage seemed set for a civil war.

In the meantime, opposition to the institution of slavery—and the Kansas-Nebraska Act in particular—mounted. One evening Anthony Burns, a runaway slave, was arrested on a false charge of robbing a jewelry store. Abolitionists raided the courthouse where Burns was being held. A crowd tried to break down the doors to rescue Burns. During the struggle, a volunteer policeman was fatally stabbed. Burns remained a prisoner.

When Pierce learned of the event, he praised the police for enforcing the law. The tragedies in his personal life seemed to have clouded his thinking. Pierce did not see the immoral side of slavery. Nor could he understand the passion of the people trying to abolish it.

CHAPTER EIGHT

ON THE WORLD STAGE

*The vast interests of commerce are
common to all mankind.*

—Franklin Pierce, from his 1853 inaugural address

Once the expansion of the continental United States had been completed, Pierce turned his attention to Cuba. Only ninety miles off the coast of Florida, Cuba seemed close enough to be part of the United States. Such a beautiful island in the Caribbean Sea would be a jewel in the country's crown, Pierce thought. There was only one problem. Spain owned Cuba.

Yet, Pierce pursued his goal. He asked three diplomats—James Buchanan, John Mason, and Pierre Soule—to meet in Ostend, Belgium, in October 1854. There, the U.S. diplomats and diplomats from Great Britain, France, and Spain discussed the purchase of Cuba from Spain. Their secret report was titled the Ostend Manifesto.

The manifesto offered to pay Spain $120 million for the

*The public feared Pierce and his diplomats planned to steal Cuba
from Spain. James Buchanan (second from right) was singled
out in this political cartoon against the Ostend Manifesto.*

purchase of Cuba. If Spain refused the offer, the United
States would go to war to take over the island. But some-
one gave a copy of the report to the U.S. press.
Northerners, especially, were outraged. Some thought that
Pierce wanted the island only as a possible source of slave
labor. (Many of Cuba's early settlers had come from Africa.)
The reaction to the Ostend Manifesto proved so damaging
to Pierce that he gave up the whole idea.

AHEAD OF HIS TIME

Pierce also hoped to add the Hawaiian Islands to the United
States. Many U.S. businesspeople had developed large sugar-
cane plantations on these faraway Pacific islands. But in the

1850s, Great Britain and France were also interested in building ties with Hawaii. Both countries plotted to crush the U.S. plan to control the Pacific islands. Many Americans thought Pierce was crazy to want to annex a country so far away from the U.S. mainland.

Pierce's plan was strongly opposed by sugar companies in the United States. They feared a loss of jobs for local workers. The bill never came up for a vote in the Senate. (More than one hundred years later, in 1959, Hawaii became the fiftieth U.S. state. Franklin Pierce's idea of annexing Hawaii proved to be a good one—and way ahead of its time.)

Next, Pierce focused on officially opening trade with the empire of Japan, an island country in the North Pacific Ocean. His efforts to do so were highly praised. For hundreds of years, Japan had been an isolationist country. It wanted no foreign traders on its shores. But Pierce was deter-

Commodore Matthew Perry's trip to Japan was a success.
Here he meets with imperial representatives.

mined to change that policy. He wanted to make U.S. ships welcome in Japan's ports. Many U.S. ships carrying goods to China could benefit by using Japanese ports in the Pacific.

Pierce organized a special mission to Japan for Commodore Matthew Perry. He was a prominent naval officer and a skilled diplomat. Perry packed samples of goods from Western culture, including telescopes and miniature models of railroads. He and his fleet left on their historic mission in 1853. The Japanese were so impressed by what they saw that Japan opened its ports to U.S. ships. Diplomatic and trade relations between Japan and the United States began.

The U.S. entrance onto the world stage had begun earlier. The country's reputation as a world leader advanced during Pierce's administration, however. Professor Gara noted, "Sparring with Great Britain, Spain, and France, forcibly opening Japan to the West, and establishing increased U.S. presence in Hawaii, Central America, and the Pacific islands demonstrated the importance of foreign policy during the years of the Pierce administration."

But all the achievements abroad could not erase the explosive issue of slavery at home. It was spinning out of control, and many people wondered how long Pierce could hold the country together. He could not possibly ignore the issue that was tearing the country apart—especially as the presidential election of 1856 approached.

DEFEAT

While Pierce focused on international matters, local rebellions over slavery increased in the United States. Pierce had hoped that the Compromise of 1850 had put the slavery issue to rest, but it hadn't. Harsher fugitive slave laws, a part of the compromise, added fuel to the debate. Still, Pierce clung to his belief in the right of states to choose slavery—a right protected by the Constitution. At the same time, he, like many Americans, was convinced that slavery would "eventually disappear."

After all the efforts to settle the territories and unite new states, Pierce could not face the possibility of a divided nation. To Pierce, holding the country together, keeping the states united, was most important of all—even if half-free and half-slave.

But the unrest in the United States was not only a case of freedom versus slavery. It was also about money and power. Two major economic sectors existed in the country. The industrialists made their money manufacturing goods in factories, mainly in the North. The plantation owners, in the South, depended on slaves to tend and harvest crops. If the South lost its slave labor, it would lose its wealth and power. Unlike white workers, black slaves weren't paid for their labor. They worked for nothing except their meager food and housing. Pierce was from the North. Though he personally did not approve of slavery, he put his faith in the Constitution. The Constitution, he often repeated, gave states the right to decide such issues. He continued to side with the southern states on their right to hold slaves.

In 1855, to quiet proslavery uprisings in Kansas, Pierce removed the territory's governor, Andrew Reeder, a north-erner. But then the North violently objected to Reeder's dismissal. Pierce had succeeded in alienating both the North *and* the South. And the feuding was not confined to Kansas. Pierce's stand against the abolitionists separated him from his former northern allies—including those in his

Pierce removed Kansas Territory governor Andrew Reeder (left) *from office after Kansas continued to have uprisings over slavery. He hoped Reeder's removal would bring peace to the new territory.*

✧ ────────────────

home state. By 1856 his chances of being reelected seemed remote at best.

By 1856 the Republican Party included former Whigs and Democrats who opposed Pierce's states' rights view of slavery. The party called for a repeal of the Kansas-Nebraska Act. It also demanded an end to slavery. As more land became available to settlers in Kansas, clashes between the southern settlers and the northern settlers grew more violent. Finally, it came time to vote on whether Kansas would be a slave territory or a free territory. Voting fraud and uprisings became widespread. Proslavery supporters from Missouri entered Kansas and voted illegally for slavery. They won the election. Kansas became a slave territory. But the Free State Party continued to fight against Kansas being a slave state. (By 1859 the antislavery leaders had triumphed and outlawed slavery in Kansas.)

THE RISE OF THE UNDERGROUND RAILROAD

When the Fugitive Slave Act went into effect, abolitionists went into action against it. But Franklin Pierce strongly supported it during his presidency. He praised federal troops who put down rebellions against the act. Keeping peace and preventing bloodshed was his mission. He did not understand the power and the passion of the people who wanted slaves to enjoy the same freedom as other U.S. citizens.

The act authorized slave owners to recapture their runaway slaves. Sympathetic northerners offered hiding places, called stations, to protect the escapees. They were determined to help slaves in the South escape from their owners and find freedom in the North. The stations were

✦ ——————————

Posters like this one circulated throughout the United States to inform citizens about the Fugitive Slave Act.

A sympathetic northerner helps a runaway slave escape. The journey on the Underground Railroad could take from two to twelve months.

usually in peoples' homes. As more and more joined the cause, the stations formed an organized network from the South to the North. Because of its secrecy, the system was named the Underground Railroad. The guides, or conductors, were men and women of great courage.

Conductors knew that if government authorities caught them aiding runaway slaves, they would be imprisoned. Still, they took the risk. If they were caught, they would serve their terms. Then they would return to their work in the Underground Railroad.

In 1852, when Pierce was elected president, the Anti-Slavery Society in Toronto, Canada, rescued about thirty thousand fugitives from the South. Many earned enough money to buy land in Canada and run their own farms.

MAKING MORE ENEMIES

In Congress, Senator Charles Sumner of Massachusetts spoke out against slavery and opposed proslavery advocate, Senator Andrew Butler of South Carolina. Congressman Preston Brooks, Butler's nephew, physically attacked Sumner on the Senate floor. Brooks beat the defenseless Sumner with his cane. He kept up the attack until the cane broke in half.

Such incidents enraged the antislavery groups. On May 24, the famous abolitionist John Brown and his followers broke into a house and murdered five proslavery settlers in Kansas. More massacres followed. Federal troops helped to bring peace

John Brown and his followers killed five proslavery settlers.

James Buchanan won the Democratic Party's nomination for president in 1856.

✧ ————————————

in the territory. By that time, however, the Democratic Party could see that Pierce's efforts to unite the country were actually dividing it. At their next convention, the Democrats wanted to nominate a more neutral candidate for the presidency. On June 2, James Buchanan became the party's nominee for president in the 1856 election.

Buchanan, Pierce's minister in Great Britain, had been far removed from all the turmoil in Kansas and throughout the country. He seemed an ideal choice. On November 4, he defeated his Republican opponent, John C. Frémont, and became the fifteenth president of the United States.

Pierce was overjoyed that the Democratic Party had regained a majority of seats in Congress and was in control of the government. Pierce sent his congratulations to Buchanan, saying, "No patriotic citizens of the Republic can have failed to breathe more deeply and freely since all doubt was removed from the result of the election. I congratulate my country and congratulate you."

*Jane Pierce's health kept her from performing many of the
duties of a First Lady during her husband's presidency.*

CHAPTER NINE

"AT MY FATHER'S FIRESIDE"

*The most . . . potent appeal for freedom will be
its own history—its trials and its triumphs.*
—Franklin Pierce, from his 1853 inaugural address

Jane Pierce looked forward to leaving the White House.
During her remaining days in Washington, she especially
enjoyed farewell visits from her sisters, Mary Aiken and
Elizabeth Packard, her aunt Nancy Lawrence, her great-aunt
Mary Mason, and all their families. Though she remained
away from people most of the time, such visits lifted her
spirits. Her niece Mary Elizabeth wrote to her mother, "I
am getting to love her very much." And Jane's loving re-
marks about Mary made her mother realize how "blessed a
treasure is a sister."

Franklin's brother, Henry, and nephews Franklin and
Kirk also visited the White House. "I desire to see you especially to converse about plans for life when my labors
here shall come to a close," Pierce wrote to his brother.

Nathaniel Hawthorne (left) *met up with the Pierces in Italy in 1857.*

Those labors came to a close on March 3, 1857, when Buchanan was inaugurated. The Pierces looked forward to a long vacation at last—far away from Washington. For the next three years, they traveled throughout Europe. While in Italy, they met Nathaniel Hawthorne and renewed their friendship. Hawthorne was surprised to see how Pierce had changed. He was stunned by "his whitening hair and furrowed face" and by "something that seemed to have passed away out of him, without leaving a trace." Wherever they went, Jane Pierce carried Bennie's Bible and a little box containing locks of his hair. His death was always present in her life.

The Pierces returned to Concord in 1859. They discovered that President Buchanan was having as tough a time as Pierce had had. Buchanan had no better luck in quieting the chaos in the country over slavery. Some Democrats urged Pierce to run again for the presidency in 1860. But he refused. He was glad to be free of the burdens of the office. Abraham Lincoln was elected president that year.

The Pierces bought a new house in Concord. They then spent the winter in Nassau, the capital of the Bahamas (a chain of islands southeast of Florida). They hoped Jane's health would improve there, but it did not. She was growing weaker and more tired. Pierce himself came down with a cold. It kept him inside and away from others. Pierce continued to brood about the state of the country. He opposed Lincoln's war policies. War could be avoided, Pierce still thought. "If we could gain a little

————————————— ✧
Abraham Lincoln (right) received only about 40 percent of the popular vote in the 1860 election.

time, there would seem to be ground of hope that these just causes of distrust and dissatisfaction might be removed," he wrote to a friend. The importance of the slavery issue seemed to escape him. Or was he just unable to cope with it?

STILL SEARCHING FOR PEACE

South Carolina seceded from the Union in December 1860. But Pierce still urged the South to act peacefully. "The Southern states must not act precipitately but give their Northern friends an opportunity to right the South's wrongs peacefully," he wrote in a letter to southern leaders. His letter was published throughout the South. But it made no difference.

However, a letter on a personal subject to President Lincoln became historic. Pierce wrote to Lincoln on the death of Lincoln's son Willie. The letter is considered one of the most moving letters ever written from one president to another. Pierce wrote:

> *The impulse to write you, the moment I heard of your great domestic affliction was very strong, but it brought back the crushing sorrow which befell me just before I went to Washington in 1853, with such power that I feel your grief to be too sacred for instruction. Even in this hour, so full of danger to our Country, and of trial and anxiety to all good men, your thoughts will be, of your cherished boy, who will nestle in your heart, until you meet in that new life, where tears and toils and conflicts will be unknown.*

14792

*Pierce wrote this letter to Abraham Lincoln after
Lincoln's son Willie died of typhoid fever in 1862.*

Pierce's own pain and sorrow never seemed to end. On December 2, 1863, Jane Pierce died. His old friend Nathaniel Hawthorne came to comfort him and accompanied him to the gravesite. Though Hawthorne had been ill most of the year, he was determined to be with his grieving friend on that cold, winter day. "The wind was penetrating," Nichols wrote, "and Pierce leaned over to wrap Hawthorne's collar more securely around his neck."

The following spring, Pierce and Hawthorne took a trip to New Hampshire's beautiful White Mountains. Pierce hoped that the mountain air would help his friend and be a

When Pierce checked on Hawthorne in the next room of this Plymouth, New Hampshire, hotel at three in the morning, the author had already died.

refreshing change for them both. But during their visit there, on May 19, 1864, Hawthorne died in his sleep of natural causes.

Pierce felt very much alone at Hawthorne's funeral. There, he stood among giants of American literature—Henry Wadsworth Longfellow, Ralph Waldo Emerson, John Whittier, and Louisa May Alcott.

THE COMFORT OF FRIENDS

Jane Pierce's death, followed by Hawthorne's, took a toll on Pierce's health. He began to drink too much despite his weakened condition. Finally, he turned to old friends for comfort and support. Pierce's health improved. Soon he was walking around town greeting people, as he had done in Washington.

Some people in Pierce's home state had turned against him because of his position on slavery. But others revered him for the many kindnesses he had shown them in the past. And many believed that Pierce had been so over-whelmed with personal tragedy that he had been unable to understand the scope of the nation's ills. To some young people, he remained an idol. Julian Hawthorne, Nathaniel's teenaged son, recalled:

> *There was a winning, irresistible magnetism in the presence of this man. Except my father, there was no man in whose company I liked to be so much as in his. I had little to say to him, and de-manded nothing more than a silent recognition from him, but his voice, his look, his gestures, his gait, the spiritual sphere of him, were delightful to*

*me; and I suspect that his rise to the highest office
in our nation was due quite as much to this
power or quality in him as to any intellectual or
executive ability that he may have possessed.
. . . He had the old-fashioned ways, the courtesy,
and the personal dignity which are not often
seen nowadays.*

Pierce liked to remind young people that not all of life's
lessons are taught in school. Many are taught while inter-

——————————— ✦ ———————————

Pierce died in his home (below) in Concord on October 8, 1869.

acting with others outside the classroom and while serving others. He had been taught lasting lessons, he said, "at my father's fireside."

In the summer of 1869, Pierce went into seclusion in his Concord home. He was suffering from edema (swelling of the body's connective tissues) and general weakness. He was too ill to go outside. Still, he enjoyed looking out his window and watching the people on the street below. Finally, at dawn on October 8, 1869, Franklin Pierce died. The president at that time, Ulysses S. Grant, proclaimed a period of mourning throughout the United States.

"To the end of his days," Professor Nichols wrote, "he always believed that [civil] war could have been avoided if there had been the same self-sacrificing devotion to the public good that carried the nation through the Revolution and made possible the adoption of the Constitution."

TIMELINE

1804 Franklin Pierce is born on November 23 in Hillsborough, New Hampshire.

1820 The U.S. Congress passes the Missouri Compromise, which settles the debate over slavery in the area of the Louisiana Purchase.

1824 Pierce graduates from Bowdoin College.

1827 Pierce is admitted to the New Hampshire bar.

1828 Pierce is elected to the New Hampshire legislature, the only representative to serve while his father was governor.

1831 Pierce is elected Speaker of the House, the youngest man to serve in that post.

1832 Pierce is elected to the U.S. Congress.

1834 Pierce marries Jane Means Appleton in Amherst, New Hampshire, on November 19.

1835 Pierce is reelected to Congress.

1836 Franklin Jr. is born on February 2 and dies three days later.

1837 Pierce is elected to the U.S. Senate.

1839 Franklin Robert (Franky) is born on August 27.

1841 Benjamin (Bennie) is born on April 13.

1842 Pierce resigns from the Senate and returns to New Hampshire.

1843 Franky dies of typhus on November 14.

1846 Pierce enlists in the Mexican War on May 25 as a private. He is quickly promoted to colonel and then brigadier general.

1850 The U.S. Congress passes the Compromise of 1850, which eases friction between the North and the South over the question of slavery.

1852 Pierce is nominated for U.S. president on June 4. He is elected on November 2.

1853 Bennie is killed in a train wreck. Pierce is inaugurated on March 4. The Gadsden Purchase treaty is signed on December 30. Matthew Perry leads the first U.S. mission to Japan.

1854 Congress passes the Kansas-Nebraska Act.
The Ostend Manifesto to purchase Cuba is drawn up.

1856 James Buchanan is elected the fifteenth U.S. president.

1857–1859 The Pierces travel abroad.

1860 Pierce turns down requests to seek the presidency in 1860.

1863 Jane Pierce dies on December 2.

1869 Franklin Pierce dies on October 8 in Concord, New Hampshire.

Source Notes

7 M. Hunter, and H. Hunter, eds., *The Presidents Speak: Inaugural Addresses of Presidents of the United States; 1795–1985* (Atlantic City: American Inheritance Press, 1985), 117.

11 Ibid., 124.

12 Roy Franklin Nichols, *Franklin Pierce* (Philadelphia: University of Pennsylvania Press, 1958), 10.

12–13 Ibid.

16 Ibid., 14.

17 Hunter and Hunter, 120.

17 Nichols, 16.

17–18 Ibid, 17.

19 Ibid., 25, 26.

19 Ibid., 27.

19–20 Ibid..

24 Gara, 2.

24–25 Nichols, 48.

25 Ibid., 50.

27 Ibid., 34,

27 Ibid, 36.

29 Hunter and Hunter, 123.

29 Nichols, 66.

31 Bradford Miller, *Returning to Seneca Falls: The First Woman's Rights Convention and Its Meaning for Men and Women Today* (Hudson, NY: Lindisfarne Press, 1995), 166.

35 Nichols, 76.

35 Ibid., 77.

35 Ibid., 78.

39 Hunter and Hunter, 120.

41 Nichols, 89.

41 Ibid.

43 Ibid., 94.

44 Ibid., 104.

47 Hunter and Hunter, 117.

47 Ibid., 122.

48 Nichols, 108.

49 Ibid., 110.

50 Ibid., 124.

50 Ibid., 125.

52 Larry Gara, *The Presidency of Franklin Pierce* (Lawrence: University Press of Kansas, 1991), 30.

54–55 David Rubel, *Mr. President: The Human Side of America's Chief Executives* (Alexandria, VA: Time-Life Books, 1998), 88.

61 Hunter and Hunter, 118.

62 Gara, 33.

63 Ibid., 35.

63 Nichols, 204.

63 Rubel, 89.

63–64 Nichols, 206.

64 Gara, 35.

65 Ibid., 36.

65 Ibid.

67 Nichols, 215.

69 Hunter and Hunter, 122.

71 Nichols, 124.

72 Joseph Krutch, ed. *Walden and Other Writing: From Slavery to Freedom*, (New York: Macmillan, 1898), 187.

72 Ibid.

72 Louis Untermeyer, ed. *A Treasury of Great Poems*, (New York: Simon & Schuster, 1942), 891.

73 Ibid.

73 John Bartlett, *Familiar Quotations* (New York: Garden City Publishing Co., Inc., 1944), 480

74 Nichols, 233.

74 Gara, 48.

74 Ibid., 40–41.

75 Nichols, 312

76 Gara, 49.

82 Hunter and Hunter, 120.

85 Gara., 156.

86 Ibid., 181.

91 Nichols, 488.
93 Hunter and Hunter, 118.
93 Carl Sferrazza Anthony, *America's First Families* (New York: Simon & Schuster, 2000), 152.
93 Ibid., 149.
94 Nichols, 508.

95–96 Ibid., 514.
96 Nichols, 515.
96 Anthony, 362.
98 Nichols, 524.
99–100 Ibid., 529.
101 Ibid., 532.
101 Ibid., 518.

Selected Bibliography

Anthony, Carl Sferrazza. *America's First Families*. New York: Simon & Schuster, 2000.

Bartlett, D. W. *The Life of General Franklin Pierce of New Hampshire: The Democratic Candidate for the Presidency of the United States*. Buffalo, NY: Auburn, Derby and Miller, 1852.

Bartlett, John. *Familiar Quotations*. New York: Garden City Publishing Co., Inc., 1944.

Daniel, Clifton, ed. *Chronicle of America*. New York: Dorling Kindersley Publishing, Inc., 1995.

Gara, Larry. *The Presidency of Franklin Pierce*. Lawrence: University Press of Kansas, 1991.

Hawthorne, Nathaniel. *Great Short Works of Nathaniel Hawthorne*. Edited by Frederick C. Crews. New York: Harper & Row Publishers, 1967.

Hunter, M., and H. Hunter, eds. *The Presidents Speak: Inaugural Addresses of Presidents of the United States: 1795–1985*. Atlantic City, NJ: American Inheritance Press, 1985.

Miller, Bradford. *Returning to Seneca Falls: The First Woman's Rights Convention and Its Meaning for Men and Women Today*. Hudson, NY: Lindisfarne Press, 1995.

Nichols, Roy Franklin. *Franklin Pierce*. Philadelphia: University of Pennsylvania Press, 1958.

Rubel, David. *Mr. President: The Human Side of America's Chief Executives*. Alexandria, VA: Time-Life Books, 1998.

Siebert, Wilbur. *The Underground Railroad: From Slavery to Freedom* New York: Macmillan, 1898.

Thoreau, Henry David. *Walden and Other Writings by Henry David Thoreau*. Edited by Joseph Wood Krutch. New York: Bantam Books, 1989.

Untermeyer, Louis, ed. *A Treasury of Great Poems*. New York: Simon & Schuster, 1955.

FURTHER READING AND WEBSITES

American Presidents: Life Portraits
http://www.americanpresidents.org.
This site contains a video showing various portraits of Pierce and related people and places.

Arnold, James R. *The Civil War*. Minneapolis: Lerner Publications Company, 2005.

Brown, Dottie. *New Hampshire*. Minneapolis: Lerner Publications Company, 2002.

Donovan, Sandy. *James Buchanan*. Minneapolis: Lerner Publications Company, 2005.

Establishing Borders: The Expansion of the United States
http://www.smithsonianeducation.org/educators/lessons_plans/borders/resources.html
This site provides additional information on the Mexican War (1846–1848), including a timeline, maps, and links to PBS (Public Broadcasting System).

Feldman, Ruth Tenzer. *The Mexican-American War*. Minneapolis: Twenty-First Century Books, 2004.

Franklin Pierce Bicentennial
http://www.Franklinpierce.ws
This is a bicentennial page-commemorating the two hundredth birthday of President Pierce, who was born on November 23, 1804.

Japan in Pictures. Minneapolis: Lerner Publications Company, 1994.

Meltzer, Milton. *Henry David Thoreau*. Minneapolis: Twenty-First Century Books, 2007.

———. *Nathaniel Hawthorne*. Minneapolis: Twenty-First Century Books, 2007.

———. *Walt Whitman*. Minneapolis: Twenty-First Century Books, 2002.

Naden, Corinne J., and Rose Blue. *Why Fight: The Causes of the American Civil War*. Austin, TX: Steck-Vaughn Company, 2000.

Questia: The World's Largest Online Library
  http://www.questia.com
  This is an online search page that directs to pages, books, journals, and encyclopedias regarding Franklin Pierce's life and presidency.

Thoreau, Henry David. *Walden, or Life in the Woods*. New York: Knopf, 1992.

The White House
  http://www.whitehouse.gov/history/presidents
  This site offers biographical information and includes photos of President Franklin Pierce.

INDEX

ABOUT THE AUTHOR

Caroline Evensen Lazo has written numerous biographies of men and women whose lives have helped to shape our own. Her works include: *Gloria Steinem: Feminist Extraordinaire; F. Scott Fitzgerald: Voice of the Jazz Age; Leonard Bernstein: In Love with Music; Harry S. Truman;* and *Frank Gehry. Alice Walker: Freedom Writer,* a Society of School Librarians International (SSLI) Honor Book, and *Arthur Ashe* were selected at Notable Social Studies Trade Books for Young People by the National Council for Social Studies.

———————— ✧ ————————

PHOTO ACKNOWLEDGMENTS

The images in this book are used with the permission of: The White House, pp. 1, 7, 11, 17, 29, 39, 47, 61, 69, 82, 93; Library of Congress, pp. 2 (LC-USZC2-2424), 6 (LC-USZC2-2363), 8, 25 (LC-USZ62-90722), 26 (LC-USZ62-5099), 28 (LC-USZ62-94061), 34 (LC-USZ62-25787), 40 (LC-USZ62-9425), 44 (LC-USZ62-47915), 48 (LC-USZ62-58516), 52 (LC-USZ62-13011), 54 (LC-USZ62-5664), 56 (LC-USZC4-4550), 57 (LC-USZ62-71730), 65 (LC-USZ62-7490), 68 (LC-USZ62-127054), 71 (LC-USZ62-4187), 78 (LC-DIG-cwpbh-00882), 80 (LC-USZ62-92043), 83 (LC-USZ62-9177), 84 (LC-USZC4-3379), 88, 94 (LC-USZ62-2358), 95 (LC-USC62-58751), 97; © Bettmann/CORBIS, pp. 10, 30, 46, 89; New Hampshire Historical Society, pp. 12 (both), 14, 16, 33, 51, 64, 66, 70, 92, 100; George J. Mitchell Dept. of Special Collections & Archives, Bowdoin College Library, Brunswick, Maine, p. 18; Laura Westlund/Independent Picture Service, pp. 21, 53; © Kean Collection/Getty Images, p. 23; © Brown Brothers, pp. 37, 43, 91; © North Wind Picture Archives, pp. 42, 55, 62, 76, 77; © CORBIS, p. 58; Courtesy of the National Archives/Newsmakers/Getty Images, p. 60; Special Collections, Ellis Library, University of Missouri-Columbia, p. 73; Picture History, p. 75; Kansas State Historical Society, p. 87; National Archives, p. 90 (520060); Peabody Essex Museum, Salem, MA, p. 98.

Cover: Library of Congress (LC-USZ62-13014).